Moby Dick

HERMAN MELVILLE

Level 2

Retold by Kathy Burke
Series Editors: Andy Hopkins and Jocelyn Potter

Pearson Education Limited
Edinburgh Gate, Harlow,
Essex CM20 2JE, England
and Associated Companies throughout the world.

ISBN 978-1-4058-8166-1

First published 2006
This edition published 2008

1 3 5 7 9 10 8 6 4 2

Text copyright © Pearson Education Ltd 2008
Illustrations by Michael Angelo P. Zarzuela

Typeset by Graphicraft Limited, Hong Kong
Set in 11/14pt Bembo
Printed in China
SWTC/01

Produced for the Publishers by
Graphicraft Productions Limited, Dartford, UK

Published by Pearson Education Limited in association with
Penguin Books Ltd, both companies being subsidiaries of Pearson Plc

For a complete list of the titles available in the Penguin Readers series please write to your local
Pearson Education office or to: Penguin Readers Marketing Department, Pearson Education,
Edinburgh Gate, Harlow, Essex, CM20 2JE

Contents

Introduction

"I'm going to finish this! I'll stop when the white devil is dead—with my harpoon in his white devil's body."

Captain Ahab hates Moby Dick—"the white devil"—because he lost a leg to the white whale in a fight. Now Ahab, the captain of a whaling ship, can only think of one thing. He has to find Moby Dick and kill him.

Many of the other sailors on the ship don't know about their captain's plan. Ishmael is a young sailor and this is his first whaling job. He and his new friend, Queequeg, sail with Captain Ahab on this exciting—and dangerous—trip. Also on the ship are Starbuck, Stubb, and other whalers from different countries. Will they find Moby Dick? What will happen next?

Herman Melville was born in 1819 in New York City. His father died when Herman was twelve. There was no money after that, so from the age of fifteen Herman had to work. He had many jobs. He worked in a bank and he was a schoolteacher. Then he began working on ships. He left New York in 1841 on his first whaling ship, the *Acushnet*. Herman loved the ocean, but whaling was a very hard life. He left the ship after eighteen months, but his life on the *Acushnet* gave him ideas for *Moby Dick* and other stories. He sailed back to the United States in 1844 and wrote books about his exciting life on the ocean. People loved them and they sold well. In 1847 he married and bought a farm. He began to write *Moby Dick* in 1850, but people didn't like it as much as his earlier books. Herman Melville moved back to New York in 1863 and died there in 1891.

Now people around the world know the story of Captain Ahab and the white whale, Moby Dick. Some people say that it is the best book in the English language.

Chapter 1   My Story Begins

He is out there—in the ocean. But he is here too—in my dreams, always in my dreams. He will never leave me. He is whiter than the first beautiful snow in winter—whiter than the stars in the sky on a warm summer's night. But he brings only death. He is Moby Dick—the white whale.

♦

My name is Ishmael and this is my story. I'm a sailor and I work on different ships. I love my life on the ocean. It's sometimes dangerous but never, never boring. I feel sad when I'm not on a ship.

One November day I thought, "I want to work on a whaling ship." Why did I want to be a whaler? I can't tell you. The life of a whaler is very dangerous. The men are away from their homes and families for years. Many never come back. Their wives wait at home. They stand and look at the ocean with sad eyes. But I wanted to visit exciting new places and I wanted to see the whales.

The first American whalers sailed from the town of Nantucket, so I went there too. I arrived on a cold, dark night and looked for a room. I was tired, so I went into the first place. The men inside drank and talked loudly. A large man with a red face stood behind the bar.

"Do you have a room for tonight?" I asked him.

"Our rooms are full," he said. "The men are here for the whaling ships. I'll have to put you in a room with Queequeg." Then he smiled and looked around at the other men.

"Who's Queequeg? Where is he?" I asked.

"Oh, he's a whaler. He's out now, but he'll be back later," said the man. Then he smiled again and the other men laughed loudly.

I didn't understand, but I was very tired. So I went to the room and got into bed. I fell asleep very quickly.

A noise outside the door woke me up. I opened my eyes but I didn't speak. The door opened and a man came in. It was dark, so I couldn't see him well. Then he lit a fire in the fireplace.

When I saw him in the light of the fire, I sat up. He was a huge man and very, very ugly! He had black lines over his face and body, and almost no hair on his head. He wore a strange skirt and no other clothes.

The huge man suddenly jumped onto my bed.

"Help!" I shouted. "Help!"

The barman ran in. "Stop, Queequeg! This man wants a bed for tonight. He's sleeping here." Then he turned to me. "This is Queequeg—the finest whaler on the ocean. Don't be afraid. He won't hurt you!" He laughed and left us.

After he left, we were very quiet. "I'm sorry," I said.

"I too," Queequeg said. His English was slow and careful.

We began to talk and then we couldn't stop! Queequeg listened to my life story and I listened to his. He came from Kokovoko, a long way away in the Pacific Ocean. He had a good life because his father was an important man. But Queequeg wanted to see the world. So he left his home and sailed away in his small boat. A whaling ship found him and gave him work. Queequeg was strong and quick so he was a fine whaler now. He never went home.

When the morning came, we were great friends. Queequeg stood up and shouted, "You will find us a whaling ship today! You and I will sail around the world!"

And do you know something? He was right! Queequeg *knew* because he could see the future. I learned this later. He was a strange and wonderful new friend.

"When the morning came, we were great friends."

Chapter 2 We Find Our Ship

That morning I looked around Nantucket for a good whaling ship. I stopped looking when I saw the *Pequod*. It was tall and strong. Its wood was dark from many years on the wild oceans.

I went onto the ship. A man sat at a table with a big book in front of him. He wore a long black coat and a big black hat. He didn't smile.

"This is a fine ship and I want to go whaling with you! Where do I write my name, Captain?" I asked happily.

"I'm not the captain. Captain Ahab is sick. He's down below. I'm Starbuck. Are you a whaler?" he asked.

"No, but I'm a good sailor," I answered. "You can ask the captains of my other ships."

"I'm not interested in your captains and your ships," he said. "Sailing is not whaling. Whaling is a hard life. You'll be away from home for many years. The work is difficult. You have to be strong and fast. And it's very dangerous."

"I want to learn. And I want to see the world," I said.

"Oh, you'll see the world. And you'll see more—good and bad. Some very bad things."

He looked at me for a minute. Then he spoke again. "I'll tell you about whaling. Captain Ahab has only one leg. And do you know why? Because a whale took his other leg. A huge whale took it off!"

I said nothing. What could I say?

"So, you want to be a whaler on Captain Ahab's ship. Can you look into the eye of a whale? Can you stand in front of its huge mouth and throw your harpoon?"

"I can and I will!" I shouted. "I'm not afraid. I'm a good sailor. You'll see! This is my life and I . . ."

He stopped me and turned the big book around. "Write your name here," he said. His eyes were tired.

"Thank you. You won't be sorry," I said.

"Don't forget my words," he answered.

"I have a friend. He's a good whaler," I said.

"We'll see. Bring him tomorrow," said Starbuck.

Queequeg and I went to the *Pequod* the next day. The men on the ship laughed at this huge, ugly man. Queequeg didn't say anything. He looked down at the water from the ship. Then he turned and spoke to the men.

"Do you see that bird?" he asked.

The men looked, but they couldn't see anything.

"There," said Queequeg.

The men looked carefully this time and saw a small dead bird a long way away on the water.

"That bird is a whale's eye," said Queequeg. He threw his harpoon and hit the bird. "Now that whale is dead," he said.

The men were quiet. Queequeq was better than every other man on that ship. And so the *Pequod* had two new whalers.

We went to our room and got our things. An old man stopped us on the street before we got back to the *Pequod*.

"Are you sailing with Captain Ahab? Do you know him?" he asked.

"Yes, we're sailing with him. He's sick now. But we'll meet him later," I answered.

"Sick!" he shouted. "Yes! He's a sick man. He's the DEVIL!"

"And who are you?" I asked.

"I'm Elijah," he answered.

"Why do you say this about Captain Ahab? Men say that he's a good whaler. He knows the ocean."

"They're right," answered the man quietly. Then his eyes turned big and wild. "But he's the DEVIL! I sailed with him. I know! And his men are the Devil's helpers!" He looked at me strangely. "He only has one leg. Do you know Captain Ahab's story?"

I suddenly felt afraid. "Of course we do," I said. I turned to Queequeg. "Come my friend," I said. "Let's leave this crazy old man." And we went quickly to the ship.

♦

We sailed on Christmas morning. Captain Ahab didn't come up and meet the whalers. But every night we heard him. He walked up and down ... up and down ...

One night we heard Starbuck speak. "Please Captain. Stop. You're waking your men up."

"No! *I* can't sleep, so my *men* won't sleep. They can think of whales in their beds—*dead* whales. That's their job!" shouted Captain Ahab.

I thought of Elijah's words: "the Devil's helpers." Were the men on the *Pequod* devils? There was unhappy Starbuck. Then there was Stubb. He was very different. He always laughed and told funny stories. From my bed I looked around at my neighbors —Bildad, Tashtego, Daggoo, Flask, Manxman, and the other whalers. They were from many different countries and had interesting stories. They weren't all good men, but they weren't devils. Who *were* Captain Ahab's devils?

Chapter 3   Captain Ahab's Story

For three weeks Captain Ahab stayed below. Then one day, suddenly, he was there in front of us. He was a thin man, but he was strong. He had a hard face with lines on it from years of sun and wind. His hair was gray and wild. His clothes were black. Then I saw it—his white whalebone leg. And an ugly white line ran down from the top of his head. Did it go down to his feet? Who—or what—did that to him? What fight did he lose so badly?

Then one day, suddenly, he was there in front of us.

He stood and looked at us with angry eyes. "What do you do when you see a whale?" he suddenly shouted.

"Shout, sir," answered the men.

"Good! Look at this!" He showed us some gold. "I want one whale—a white whale. One of you will see this whale first! That man will get this gold!"

We stood quietly. Whalers don't make much money. We thought about the gold. We could buy a lot of nice things with it.

"You'll know him when you see him," said Captain Ahab. "He's the biggest whale in the oceans."

"I saw this whale," said Queequeg to me. "He is a mountain! Very big. Very strong. I put my harpoon in him. He got away!"

"I have to find this whale! I WILL find him!" shouted Captain Ahab.

"Are you talking about Moby Dick?" asked Tashtego.

"Yes!" answered Captain Ahab.

"Moby Dick took your leg?" said Starbuck quietly.

Captain Ahab shouted angrily at Starbuck. "Yes! He took my leg. He took half of me. Now I'm half a man. And Moby Dick will pay for this! I'll follow him to South America, to Africa. I'll follow him to the end of this world. I'll see him dead!" He turned to the other whalers. "Are you with me, men?"

"Yes!" they shouted. They were excited. They saw the gold! They shouted and laughed.

Only Starbuck stood quietly. His face was as dark as the sky before it rains.

"What's your problem?" Captain Ahab asked him angrily. Then he smiled. "It's too dangerous. Is that the problem?"

"I'm not afraid of dangerous work," answered Starbuck. "But I work for whale oil. I fight whales for their oil—for money. You hate this whale. How much oil will that bring you? How much money?"

"When I kill Moby Dick, I'll be rich in here!" shouted Captain Ahab and he hit his body with his hand. He turned and started to walk away.

"Are you going to follow this animal because it won a fight with you? It's wrong. It's crazy!" shouted Starbuck.

When he heard this, Captain Ahab turned on his whalebone leg. He was very angry now and he shouted in Starbuck's face.

"This whale is *evil*. Do you understand? White is the color of ice and ice takes strong ships down under the water. White is the color of a man's eyes when he can't see. White is the color of dead men. White is evil and this whale is evil. He's laughing at me. I'll only be free when this evil is dead! Dead!"

The color left Starbuck's face. He was the loser of this fight and Captain Ahab knew it. He turned to the men again.

"Drink! Death to Moby Dick!" he shouted.

The men put their harpoons up high and shouted too. Then they drank and danced.

♦

Later that same night the men were asleep and the ship was quiet. I was outside with Pip, the little cook boy. We had to put water out for the next day's whaling.

"Listen," said Pip. "Can you hear that? I hear men."

The whalers were at the other end of the ship. There was nobody there.

"I don't hear anything," I said.

"No, listen!" said Pip. "There are men below us—five or six of them. Can't you hear them?"

"It's the ocean, Pip. It's playing games with you," I answered.

"I have good ears," said Pip. He was angry with me and walked away.

I watched him go. Then I sat and looked up at the stars. I dreamed of the white whale. I dreamed of gold.

Chapter 4   Our First Whale

"Whale!" shouted Tashtego from the top of the ship. "Whale!" Captain Ahab came quickly. "Get the boats!" he shouted. The whale sent a shower of water up into the sky.

Suddenly five men came up from below and stood by Captain Ahab. Their faces were dark and they had long black hair. They wore strange wide pants and no shirts or shoes. One of the men was older. He was darker and only had one tooth. He wore a strange white hat, so we couldn't see his hair. His black eyes looked only at Captain Ahab. These were Captain Ahab's devils!

"Fedallah! Go!" Captain Ahab shouted to this man.

Three small boats went down into the water. Captain Ahab's men came too, in their boat. His men were strong and their boat quickly sailed in front of ours.

I turned to Pip. "I understand now! These are the men! You heard them speaking before!"

"I told you!" Pip shouted back.

"Stop talking and row!" shouted Stubb from the back. "Do you think this is a tea party?" Stubb always shouted at us—but we were never afraid of him. He always had a smile on his face.

Starbuck was the captain of our small boat. He didn't talk to us, but we heard him say quietly, "Who are those men? What's Captain Ahab doing?"

Captain Ahab shouted to his boat from the *Pequod*, but his men only had ears for Fedallah. Their eyes never left Fedallah's face and their boat went faster and faster.

This was my first whale! "Maybe we'll kill it!" I thought. I was excited. Every whaler was excited. But why weren't we afraid? Because our heads were full of money—oil—gold!

The sky suddenly turned dark with rain, but we didn't go back.

"We have time. We can kill a whale before the heavy rain comes," said Starbuck.

These were Captain Ahab's devils!

Queequeg stood ready with his harpoon in the front of our boat. Suddenly the whale was there again. It came up out of the water—under our boat! Men and harpoons went everywhere. Then the heavy rain came. In minutes our boat was full of water. Strong winds took our sails down. The whale left us and swam down into the dark water.

After some time the wind stopped. We waited, and day turned to night. We couldn't see anything. Where were we? Where were the other boats? The men weren't angry with Starbuck. The weather can play games with the best sailors.

More hours came and went. We were wet, tired, and afraid. Then we saw a large black thing in the water. Was it the whale again? No! It was the *Pequod*. But the men couldn't see us!

"It's going to hit us!" shouted Stubb. We jumped into the ocean and began to shout for help. When the men on the *Pequod* heard us, they put ropes down. Then they helped us onto the ship. The other men were there—Captain Ahab's men too. They turned back when they didn't see the white whale.

Chapter 5   The *Albatross* and the *Samuel Enderby*

We fought and killed many whales after that first night. But our work didn't finish when we killed them. We then had to climb down onto the dead whale and cut off the fat. We had to work quickly because sharks came for the whale meat. Sharks could eat a whale in one night, and some of these whales were almost as big as our ship.

We cut off large squares of fat and pulled these squares onto the ship. This was a long, hard job. It was also dangerous because sharks swam around us. We then cooked the fat and made oil. When the oil was ready, we put it into barrels.

Oil gave us light and made us warm. We could sell it to people around the world. Oil was our money. But did this make Captain Ahab happy? No. The money wasn't important to him. He only thought about Moby Dick. He could only hate. He stood for hours on the ship—in the rain, in the snow—and looked at the ocean. When other ships went past, he didn't ask them, "How are you? Do you want help?" He only asked, "Did you see the white whale?"

One day we met the *Albatross*. It was on its trip home after four long years on the ocean. The ship and its whalers looked ready for home. The men were tired and thin, with large, hungry eyes.

The wind was strong that day, so the *Albatross* couldn't come near us. But the captain put his hand up and smiled. Captain Ahab shouted from the *Pequod*, "Did you see the white whale?"

The captain shouted his answer, but the wind carried his words away. Captain Ahab put his hand behind his ear, but he couldn't hear the captain.

"Aghhhh! This wind!" he shouted. "Listen! Tell people at home we're sailing around the world. We'll bring back the teeth of the devil whale!"

Starbuck stood and watched Captain Ahab. "Is he forgetting his wife and child at home?" he said to me.

"Wife and child?" I asked. Did Captain Ahab really have a family?

"Oh, yes. His family is waiting for him," said Starbuck. "And *my* family is waiting for *me*. Every day my wife, Mary, takes our son to the beach. They look at the ocean. They hope that they'll see our sails one day."

I thought about the other men on our ship. How many of these men had families? What did they leave behind them when they went on the whaling ships? Who waited for them?

"Nobody's waiting for me," I thought. "I want a wife and child. I'd like to go home to them."

◆

Day after day nothing changed. Captain Ahab always asked other ships about the white whale. Some captains knew about Moby Dick. Some laughed at Captain Ahab. "Moby Dick is only a whalers' story—nothing more!" they said.

Then one day we met the *Samuel Enderby*. The ocean was quiet and the captain, Captain Boomer, came onto our ship. He was a friendly man and smiled at us. He only had one arm.

"Did Moby Dick take your arm?" Captain Ahab asked excitedly.

"Yes, I lost my arm to the white whale," the captain answered.

Captain Ahab's face lit up. He was happy! "Come with me! The white devil will pay for your arm and my leg!" he shouted happily.

"Oh, no. I can't do that," the captain answered. "One arm is better than no arms or legs! I want my life! I think I'll leave Moby Dick in the ocean."

"*Leave* him!" shouted Captain Ahab. He turned his back to Captain Boomer for a minute. Then he turned around and shouted at him. "Get off my ship! You're afraid! *I'm* not afraid. I'll find Moby Dick. I'll look him in the eye! I'll kill him!"

The smile left Captain Boomer's face. "I hope—for you and for your men—that you never find Moby Dick."

And without another word he left our ship.

Chapter 6   Moby Dick

Captain Ahab didn't sleep very often now. We saw the light from his room on many nights. He sat at his table. He looked at his maps and planned. Where was Moby Dick? How could we find him? He only talked to Fedallah. We could hear the two men in Captain Ahab's room. Captain Ahab often shouted angrily, but Fedallah always spoke quietly. Fedallah was different from other

He looked at his maps and planned.

men. He stayed away from the other whalers. He sat high up in the sails at night and watched for whales. He slept in the day.

"Why does he watch for whales at night?" we asked. "Does he have the eyes of a cat? Can he see in the dark?"

And why did Captain Ahab only listen to this man? Fedallah wasn't God.

"He can see the future," said some whalers.

Could Fedallah really see the future? What did he see? What did he tell Captain Ahab?

One night Starbuck found Captain Ahab asleep at his table, with the light on and his maps around him.

"Crazy old man," he said quietly. "You sleep tonight, but your dreams are full of your white whale. You hate Moby Dick and you're taking me and our men with you. To what? Our deaths?"

That same night we heard Fedallah. "The white whale!" he shouted.

I ran and woke the other men. We looked up and saw Fedallah at the top of the sails. He looked out at the ocean and showed us the whale. "There!" he shouted.

Suddenly a huge shower of water went up. Then a second shower. We could see something white on the water. It *was* a white whale! Was it Captain Ahab's white whale? Now we understood. Fedallah watched at night because you could see a *white* whale at night.

Captain Ahab was there. His face was as happy as a child's face on Christmas morning. "Put the sails up! Faster!" he shouted.

The white whale sent three more showers of water high up into the sky. The water looked beautiful in the light of the stars.

"Follow him!" shouted Captain Ahab.

We started to go after the whale, but it quickly swam under the water. We lost it.

"Was that really Moby Dick?" I asked Queequeg. "Will we see him again?"

Queequeg cleaned his harpoon and looked at the ocean. "He will come again," he said.

And he did. He came the next night. And the night after that —always at the same time.

"He wants me to follow him," said Captain Ahab on the third night. "He's showing us the way."

I was suddenly very afraid. We had to stay with Captain Ahab to the end. We couldn't leave. I couldn't change my future now.

Chapter 7   Pip's Story

You met our cook's boy, Pip, earlier in my story. Pip was a young black American boy. He was only fourteen. A whaling ship wasn't a nice place for a boy, but Pip liked his work. He sang in the kitchen when he helped the cook. But things changed for him.

After many weeks we lost Moby Dick and we started to look for other whales again. One of Stubb's men broke his arm, so he couldn't row. Stubb put Pip in our boat on the next whaling trip because there was no other man. Pip didn't want to go. We could see that in his face. But he always wanted to help, so he went quietly. Our first trip was fine and Pip felt happier at the end of it.

On our second trip Tashtego's harpoon hit a whale behind its eye. The angry whale turned around and hit the boat. Pip jumped up—and then out of the boat!

When he jumped, the harpoon rope caught him. The whale started to swim away fast. It pulled Pip behind it. We could see Pip's head go in and out of the water.

"Stupid boy!" shouted Tashtego. He stood up with his knife. He could cut the rope and free the boy.

He looked at Stubb. Stubb liked the boy, but he didn't want to lose the whale.

"Cut the rope!" shouted Starbuck angrily.

Tashtego cut the rope and the whale swam away. They pulled Pip back into the boat. The men were very angry with him.

"Never jump out of the boat again!" said Stubb. "We'll have to leave you. Who will bring us more money—you or a whale?"

On the third trip Pip jumped again when a whale hit the boat. He was a young boy—a cook—not a whaler. He was afraid. This time Stubb left him in the ocean.

"Please come back!" Pip shouted. "Please don't leave me! The sharks will eat me!"

But the boat went after the whale. Pip was in the ocean for a long time. The water was as cold as ice and Pip was afraid. The ocean was very dangerous.

Stubb sent the *Pequod* for him after we got our whale. When Pip climbed the rope, Captain Ahab put out his hand to him. Pip was a little crazy now. When he saw Captain Ahab's hand, he saw the hand of God.

"Thank you, God!" he cried.

After that day Pip was a different person. He followed Captain Ahab everywhere. He was always with him. And Captain Ahab was a different man when he was with Pip. He never shouted at him. He smiled and was kind to him.

After many days of this Starbuck got angry and shouted at Pip. "Captain Ahab is *not* God! Stop following him, you crazy boy!"

"Why are you angry? The boy doesn't understand," I said to Starbuck.

"I'm not angry. I'm afraid. I know the boy is crazy. But Captain Ahab? Does *he* think he's God? Is *he* . . . ?" He stopped before he said the word "crazy." "This is *not* good. It's wrong!" said Starbuck. Then he walked away.

"Please don't leave me!"

Chapter 8   Queequeg's Coffin

Some days later we heard shouts from below: "Captain! Captain Ahab!"

It was Starbuck. He ran to Captain Ahab—very fast. Starbuck was a young man. When you saw his black clothes and sad face, you could forget that.

"What is it?" Captain Ahab asked him.

"The barrels, Captain. There's a problem with some of the barrels. We're losing oil! We have to stop the ship. The men have to change the bad barrels."

"I'm not going to lose a day's sailing because of some barrels. No. We're not going to stop," answered Captain Ahab.

"But—Captain! We're losing a lot of oil!" Starbuck shouted. The men stopped working and watched. "You have to stop! We'll lose everything!"

"No! We're very near Moby Dick. I can feel it. We have to find him," answered Captain Ahab.

Starbuck was afraid. We could see this in his face. But he was very angry too. He didn't leave.

"But the men! Our wives and children! We're here because we want food for our families. The money from the oil is important to us. We have to live. We *want* to live! Where are you taking us? What are you *doing* to us?"

Captain Ahab took out his gun. "Oil is not my God! We will *not* stop!" he shouted. "Do you understand?!"

Not one man spoke. Nobody moved. We stood and watched. Starbuck slowly turned from the gun and started to walk away. "I can't win this fight," he said. "You have the gun." Then he turned around and looked at Captain Ahab. He spoke quietly.

"But be careful, Captain Ahab. Not of me—I'm not the problem. *You* are." He turned and walked away. Captain Ahab didn't speak. He watched Starbuck go. Then he put his gun down and went to his room.

Later that day Captain Ahab shouted for the men to come to him. "Starbuck says we have a problem with some of the barrels." he said. "We're going to stop and change them. Take down the sails."

Starbuck's face was happy. He didn't speak, but his eyes said "thank you."

◆

We worked day and night on the barrels. It was very hot below and oil was everywhere. The barrels were very heavy and only the strongest men could move them. Queequeg had to do a lot of this hard, heavy work. After three days we finished. The men were tired and some were sick from the work. Queequeg slept outside that night. He wanted to get away from the hot rooms below. But it was very cold outside.

The next morning Queequeg was very sick. His body was as cold as ice one minute and then as hot as fire. He couldn't see. He couldn't speak.

I stayed with him. "I'm here," I said. "My dear friend, I won't leave you. You'll get better."

After two days Queequeg called the other men to his bed. "Make me a coffin," he said. "I am going to die."

"No! You aren't going to die! You can't leave me!" I cried.

"Yes, my friend. I am going to die. Men, please make my coffin. Do not throw my body into the cold ocean."

The men made Queequeg his coffin. When they finished it, they brought it to him.

"Bring my harpoon," he said. "And some food and water." We put his harpoon next to him and brought him food and water.

"Put them in my coffin," he said. So we put them in.

"Now put me in the coffin," he said.

"No!" we shouted.

"I want to try it," he said. So we put him inside and closed it.

After some minutes he spoke. "It is good. Now I will go to my bed again."

He looked at the coffin from his bed. Then he closed his eyes and slept.

I sat and cried. I waited. The other men were very sad too. Queequeg was a good man—and the best whaler on the ocean.

Then one morning Queequeg sat up. "I cannot die now," he said. "I have to do some things first. I will die later. Now I will go to work."

Nobody could understand! But we put his coffin away—down with the barrels of oil—and went back to our work.

Chapter 9   Captain Ahab's Dream

We sailed into the Pacific Ocean and the whaling was good. One day we killed four whales. We couldn't cut the fat off four whales in one day, so we had to watch them that night.

We put the small boats into the water near the dead whales. I was in Captain Ahab's boat. We put harpoons into the whales' bodies. Then we put lights on the end of the harpoons so we could see sharks in the water.

"Shark! Shark!" men shouted from the different boats.

Sometimes only three or four came. Sometimes a lot of sharks came at the same time. They were fast and quiet. Suddenly they were there—by our boats! Their ugly mouths opened and they showed their teeth. We fought them and they went away. But they always came back again. Sometimes they stayed away for hours. In those quiet times Captain Ahab and his men slept. But Fedallah didn't sleep—he watched for sharks.

Suddenly Captain Ahab woke up and sat up in the boat. His eyes were big and wild. He was afraid!

"I had the dream again!" he said to Fedallah. "I died! I felt it! And I saw my coffin!"

"You will not have a coffin," said Fedallah. "I told you this. You know this."

"So am I going to die on the ocean?" Captain Ahab asked. "Will I die on this trip? Will I die before I kill the white whale?"

Fedallah's black eyes looked at Captain Ahab. He spoke quietly to him. "Only a rope can kill you."

"A rope? But how? What do you mean? Ah! Then I'll die when I go home! They'll put a rope around me and kill me there! Am I right?"

Fedallah spoke again. "A rope will kill you. But I will go first. I will show you the way. You will follow me to the next world."

"But when? When will this happen, Fedallah? And where?" asked Captain Ahab.

"I cannot say. I will die first. And you will follow me."

I listened carefully to the two men. Now I understood! Fedallah was important to Captain Ahab because he *could* see the future! The whalers were right! This strange man knew about Captain Ahab's death—and Captain Ahab could only die *after* Fedallah died.

Fedallah suddenly looked at me. Could he understand my thoughts? I quickly closed my eyes.

The next day, on the *Pequod*, Captain Ahab threw his maps into the ocean. "You don't help me!" he shouted. "Can you find the white whale? Do I see him in front of me now? I'll find him without you!"

Some of the men saw this. Their mouths were open and their eyes were large.

I looked at Starbuck. His face was white.

"How can a ship sail without maps?" he said. "Only a crazy man throws his maps away."

The men were afraid and that night in their beds they talked about Captain Ahab. "What's he doing? This is very dangerous. Bad things will happen now."

Then it came—the wind. One minute the ocean was quiet. Suddenly the ship was on top of a mountain of water—then down again. Up and down. Up and down. We couldn't stand. This wind took our sails down. Some of the sails hit our little whaling boats. We couldn't think. We couldn't move. Our ship danced on the wild ocean.

Captain Ahab shouted at the sky. "Are you trying to kill me? You can't! I'll fight you!"

Starbuck shouted at Captain Ahab, "God wants us to turn back! Look around you! Look at the boats! Look at our ship!"

Captain Ahab ran and got his harpoon. "No man will turn this ship around. I'll put this harpoon through that man! We'll follow Moby Dick! He lives here—in this ocean. He took my leg from me here. Now I'll find him and I'll finish our fight. He took my life and now I'll take his!"

After many hours the wind stopped. Starbuck went to Captain Ahab's room. He looked very angry. I wanted Starbuck to be our captain. I followed him and watched.

He opened Captain Ahab's door quietly. The Captain was asleep at his table. There were no maps there now, but there was a gun on the table. Starbuck slowly and carefully took the gun. He stood with it in his hand and looked at Captain Ahab.

"What can I do?" he asked quietly. "I can kill him. Then we can go home to our families." He stood for a minute before he spoke again. "Or I can leave him. Then he'll kill everyone on this ship. We'll die a long, long way from home."

I wanted Starbuck to kill Captain Ahab.

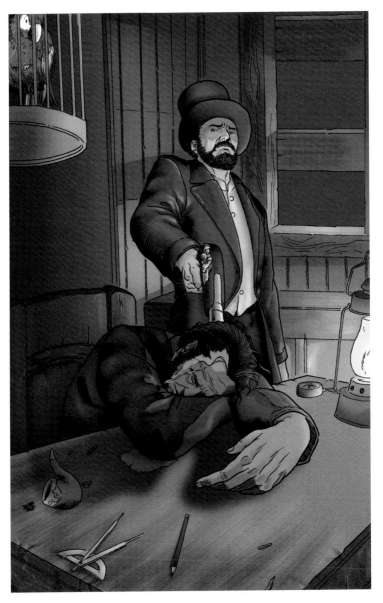

"I can kill him. Then we can go home to our families."

After some time Starbuck's hand fell. He couldn't do it. He put the gun on the table and quietly left Captain Ahab's room.

♦

The next morning we heard strange noises. What were they? Were they the sounds of animals or fish? Was it the wind? Were they the calls of dead sailors?

It was Pip. He jumped up and down. "It's me!" he cried. "I'm in the ocean! You forgot me! Help me!"

Captain Ahab went to the boy. "Don't be afraid," he said. "You're with me. Nothing will hurt you."

"Look at that," said Stubb. "Two crazy people on a crazy ship. What will happen next?"

Chapter 10   The *Rachel*

Later that day our ship met the *Rachel*. The *Rachel* looked as bad as the *Pequod* after the strong winds. But Captain Ahab didn't talk to the *Rachel*'s captain about the weather. He asked the same question: "Did you see the white whale?"

When Captain Gardiner answered, Captain Ahab jumped.

"Yes," our visitor said. "I saw him yesterday."

Captain Gardiner came onto the *Pequod* with some of his men. Captain Ahab was full of questions.

"You saw Moby Dick yesterday? Where? Did you kill him? Where is he now?"

Captain Gardiner's face went white and he began his story.

"I had three boats on the water. Suddenly the white whale came out of the ocean. I sent one of the boats after it. The men harpooned the whale. It swam away and pulled the boat after it. It was too fast! We couldn't follow the boat and we lost it. We looked last night and this morning. But we couldn't find it."

"Something on that boat is important to him," Queequeg said quietly to me.

"Maybe it's his best boat," said Daggoo.

"Or his best harpooner," said Stubb.

Captain Gardiner's face was very sad. He asked Captain Ahab, "Will you help us look for the boat, Captain?"

When Captain Ahab didn't answer, Captain Gardiner spoke again. "I'll pay you for your time."

There was no answer.

"My son was on that boat," Captain Gardiner said. "He's my only son—twelve years old. You and I can find him, Captain Ahab. I hope you'll help me."

We stood and waited for Captain Ahab's answer.

"We have to help him," said one whaler loudly. "We're all whalers and many of us have sons."

"Can't we help him?" asked another man.

"No, I can't do it," answered Captain Ahab. "We don't have time." He turned and spoke to Starbuck. "Get these men off my ship now! We are going to sail in five minutes!" Then he walked away.

Captain Gardiner looked at each whaler's face with his sad, red eyes. But we could do nothing. We had to go with our crazy captain.

♦

In the days after we met the *Rachel*, Captain Ahab started to get ready for the fight with Moby Dick. He wanted to look after Pip, so he brought Pip to his room. He spoke to him.

"These next days are going to be very dangerous," he said. "We're going to kill the white whale. This is going to be a long, hard fight. I want you to stay here—in my room, Pip. Never leave. You'll hear many things, but you have to stay here. Do you understand?"

27

Pip listened carefully to Captain Ahab. He didn't really understand everything but he always wanted to please his captain. He never left Captain Ahab's room again.

Captain Ahab always stayed outside after that. He didn't go to his room. He sat and watched the ocean for Moby Dick—morning and night. He ate outside and slept outside in his dirty clothes.

Fedallah was there too, but the two men never spoke now. They only did one thing. They watched.

♦

One morning a large black bird flew down from the sky. It flew to Captain Ahab's head! Captain Ahab put his hands up, but the bird flew around and around his head. Fedallah did nothing. Then suddenly, the bird took Captain Ahab's hat and flew away. Some of the whalers laughed. But some of them were afraid and talked about it later. "What does this mean? Will more bad things happen now?" they asked.

Chapter 11   The Fight Begins

Some days later Captain Ahab and Starbuck stood and watched for whales.

Captain Ahab spoke sadly to Starbuck. "What kind of life do I have?" he said. "Forty years of hard work, little sleep, little money. I married my dear wife and the next day I left on a whaling ship for three years! I feel old, Starbuck, old and tired. I think of my family. My young son is sleeping now."

"My son is sleeping too," answered Starbuck. "Why don't we go home and see our boys, Captain?"

Then, suddenly, Captain Ahab's face changed. "Wait! Moby Dick is near—very, very near. I can feel him!"

The hope left Starbuck's face, and it turned sad again. He walked slowly away from Captain Ahab and went back to work.

♦

Captain Ahab was right. Moby Dick was very near.

"White whale! White whale!" the Captain shouted the next morning.

And there he was—the largest and most dangerous animal in the ocean. But at this minute he was beautiful. When he came up out of the water, his great white body shone in the morning sun. Birds followed him and flew above him.

Captain Ahab's face shone too. He was a child again—happy and excited. "Get the boats, men! *Move!*" he shouted.

We didn't have many boats after the strong winds. Captain Ahab and his men climbed into the first boat.

Captain Ahab spoke to Starbuck before he left. "Stay here," he said. "Then you can see your wife and child again."

Now we were in the boats. Moby Dick came up out of the water again. He was a huge, white mountain! There were harpoons in his body from his many fights with whalers. When he hit the ocean again, water showered down on us.

Then he swam down into the dark water and the ocean was quiet. Where was he?

We sat for hours in our boats and waited.

Suddenly Tashtego shouted, "The birds! Look!"

The birds were above us, so Moby Dick was near. We looked into the water.

Something was down there. It came nearer. It got bigger ... and bigger ...

Then he was there—the huge white whale. He came up under Captain Ahab's boat! His mouth opened. I could see his teeth!

He closed his mouth on Captain Ahab's boat and took it out of the water!

Fedallah and his men jumped into the ocean. Captain Ahab didn't jump. He stayed in the boat and shouted at Moby Dick. He tried to fight him, but he couldn't. His harpoon was in the ocean now and he couldn't move easily with his whalebone leg.

Then the boat broke and fell into the ocean. But Moby Dick didn't swim away. He started to swim around Captain Ahab and his boat. He began slowly. Then he swam faster and faster. We couldn't get near him in the other boats. We couldn't help Captain Ahab.

"That whale is playing with him!" said Stubb.

The birds flew around and around in the sky above Moby Dick.

"Get the whale! Bring the *Pequod*!" shouted Captain Ahab.

The noise from the ocean and the birds was very loud. Could anybody on the *Pequod* hear him? But the *Pequod's* sails went up. It turned and started to sail to the white whale.

We watched from our boats. "It's going to hit Moby Dick!" we shouted.

But suddenly Moby Dick went down into the water again. The water stopped moving. The ocean was quiet.

Moby Dick didn't come back. The whalers on the *Pequod* pulled Captain Ahab and his men out of the water. Captain Ahab's men were really afraid now! They shouted and cried. But Fedallah didn't speak. He walked away and looked out at the ocean. How did he feel? His cold black eyes showed nothing.

Captain Ahab went to his room and got the gold.

"This gold is mine now!" he shouted to the whalers. "I saw Moby Dick first! But I'll give it away! We *will* kill Moby Dick. The only question is: when? Who will see the white devil first on that day? That man will get this gold!"

Starbuck shouted at Captain Ahab: "Didn't you learn anything today? Are you really crazy? You have to stop! Don't go after that whale again!"

"Ha!" Captain Ahab answered. "Today was nothing! *You* are

He stayed in the boat and shouted at Moby Dick.

nothing. I'm going to finish this! I'll stop when the white devil is dead—with my harpoon in his white devil's body!"

Chapter 12   The Second Day

"White whale! White whale!"

Moby Dick came again. He was hundreds of meters away, but we could see the shower of water from his back, high in the sky. He came out of the ocean. Then his huge body fell again and hit the water.

Three boats went after him. Captain Ahab and his men took Daggoo's boat. In an hour the boats were all in different places around Moby Dick. Our harpoons rained down on him. Some fell into the ocean. Some hit him and stayed in his body. The harpoon ropes pulled our boats nearer to him.

Suddenly Moby Dick started swimming round and round! He opened and closed his huge mouth. He pulled hard on the ropes and the three boats moved nearer.

Flask's boat hit ours! Wood and harpoons went everywhere. We swam quickly and tried to get away from the whale.

Moby Dick went down under the water. Where was he? How many meters could he swim with our harpoons and ropes in him? We waited.

He came up again—under Captain Ahab's boat! The boat broke and the men fell into the ocean. You could hear them shout and cry.

Then Moby Dick stopped moving. He stayed there and watched us. It was the strangest thing! He looked at us with his small black eye. We waited. Then he swam away quietly. Our harpoon ropes followed him in the water.

We waited for the *Pequod*. We had to be very careful. We didn't shout because we didn't want sharks to see us.

When they pulled me out of the water, I was happy and excited. I didn't die! But the other men? Queequeg! Where was Queequeg? Then I saw him. And Stubb? Yes, he was there too —and Tashtego, Flask, and Daggoo. But where was Captain Ahab?

After some time we heard a shout. It was Captain Ahab. His arm was around Starbuck because he couldn't walk. He had no whalebone leg now. He was tired and wet, and looked very old.

"Give me a harpoon!" he shouted angrily. "That will be my second leg for now!"

He walked with the harpoon to the men and sat down on a barrel. Then he spoke to us.

"Watch carefully," he said. "Moby Dick will come to us on the third day. He'll die on the third day. Who will see him first? Who will get the gold?"

We didn't shout and dance this time. We were tired. We were afraid. We stood quietly.

Captain Ahab looked around at us and his face suddenly changed. "Where's Fedallah?" he asked.

We looked around. He wasn't there. Nobody spoke.

Captain Ahab's face went white. His eyes were large and black. He opened his mouth, but nothing came out. Then he spoke again, but the sound was different. It was high and strange.

"Find Fedallah! Do you hear me? FIND HIM!"

We looked everywhere, but we couldn't find Fedallah.

"Maybe he went down with the ropes," said Stubb.

Stubb wasn't sad. The whalers weren't sad. Captain Ahab's men weren't sad. Only one man on that ship wanted to see Fedallah again—the Captain. He could lose his maps—and his whalebone leg—but not Fedallah.

He shouted at the ocean. "You'll die for this! My harpoon will end your evil life!"

I remembered Fedallah's words to Captain Ahab: "I will go first. I will show you the way. You will follow me from this world."

Chapter 13   The End

On the morning of the third day the sun shone in the blue sky and the ocean shone in the sunlight. The *Pequod* sailed well. It was the most beautiful day, but the saddest day.

"On the third day he'll come," Captain Ahab said again and again.

He sat high up in the sails and watched. He looked better now. He looked strong again.

After forty years on the ocean Captain Ahab understood whales well. "Why don't we see him? Ah! We're going too fast," he said. "Moby Dick has our harpoons and ropes in him. He can't swim fast. Turn around. We'll go back for him."

"Look at Captain Ahab. He's running to his death," said Starbuck sadly.

"There he is!" shouted Captain Ahab after two hours.

And there was Moby Dick.

Starbuck spoke quietly. "How are you, Mary? How's our boy?"

Why did he speak to his wife? Did he know something? Was this the end?

Captain Ahab thought only of Moby Dick. He shouted happily at the whale: "You and I had to meet. We had to fight. Now is our time!"

Captain Ahab climbed down from the sails. He couldn't walk without his whalebone leg, so Starbuck helped him.

"Will you watch our ship when I fight Moby Dick?" Captain Ahab asked Starbuck.

"Captain, don't go," said Starbuck.

"Take my hand," said Captain Ahab. "Can we be friends now —at the end?"

"Oh, Captain!" Starbuck cried.

We only had one whaling boat now, so many men had to stay on the ship. Queequeg stayed, but I had to go on the boat with Captain Ahab and the other men.

"Be careful, my friend," Queequeg said to me.

When our boat went down to the water, we saw young Pip's face in the window of Captain Ahab's room. His eyes were large and sad. He shouted to Captain Ahab, "Please don't go! Please don't leave me!"

We sat in our boat all day. The men didn't speak. Captain Ahab didn't speak. We watched and waited.

Then the water began to move.

"It's time," said Captain Ahab. "Get ready for the greatest fight of your lives."

Moby Dick came to the top of the water. Then he slowly swam to our boat. He swam near us for some minutes. Then, suddenly, he turned his body around and hit the boat hard. It broke and water started to come in. We got down on the floor of the boat and tried to stop the water.

Then Captain Ahab suddenly cried, "Aghhhh!"

In front of us was Fedallah! We could see our ropes around Moby Dick's body and Fedallah's dead body was in the ropes. One of Fedallah's arms was free. It went up and down when the whale swam past us. His eyes were open and water came out of his mouth.

We stood up. We wanted to run away, but we were in the boat.

"Sit DOWN!" Captain Ahab shouted at us. "Don't leave this boat or I'll throw a harpoon at you! ROW!"

Captain Ahab tried to stand up in the boat, but he couldn't with only one leg. "Give me a harpoon!" he said angrily.

Moby Dick slowed down again and waited. Did this animal *think*? Did it plan?

Captain Ahab spoke again. "Row near him. Don't speak. Don't make a sound."

When we went near, the whale sent up showers of water. The water rained down on us. We couldn't see, but we were very near. I put out my hand and felt his cold body!

Captain Ahab threw his harpoon. The whale moved when it hit his body. It hurt him. He was angry. He turned and hit the boat again. I fell into the water. Our sails were up and the wind carried the boat away. I shouted, but the boat couldn't stop. They had to leave me there in the water.

The boat sailed fast. The water came in and the men tried to stop it. Captain Ahab's eyes were on the ocean. He didn't see Moby Dick come again.

Flask suddenly shouted, "The ship! Moby Dick's going to hit the *Pequod*!"

"Row! Help the ship!" shouted Captain Ahab.

The men rowed as quickly as they could. I saw Queequeg on the *Pequod*. He was at the top of the sails. I saw the other men too. When they saw Moby Dick, they ran away. Some of them jumped from the ship, but Queequeg didn't move. He stayed there and watched the whale.

Moby Dick hit the *Pequod*. The noise was very loud. Then everything went quiet. Water ran through the ship.

I could hear Starbuck. He shouted at Captain Ahab, "You did this to us, Captain Ahab! God help us!"

Then I saw Daggoo and Stubb. Stubb took off his coat and shoes so he could swim.

Moby Dick didn't swim away. He waited. Then he swam between the *Pequod* and the whaling boat. The men in the boat looked at Captain Ahab. He looked old and tired, but his head was high. He spoke to the men.

"The *Pequod*'s going down," he said. "It's the best ship in this ocean and I'm not with my ship. That's very sad. A good captain has to be with his ship at the end." Then Captain Ahab's face was suddenly angry. He slowly brought his harpoon up. When he talked to the white whale, his face was the face of the Devil.

"You can kill me, but you CANNOT WIN!"

He threw the harpoon hard and fast. It hit Moby Dick below his small black eye. The whale turned and swam fast. He pulled the small boat behind him at the end of the harpoon rope. The men fell down in the boat.

Captain Ahab took out his knife and tried to cut the rope. But before he could cut it, the rope went around his body. It pulled him up and out of the boat! One minute he was there— the next minute he wasn't. There was no shout—no cry—not one word.

Suddenly the rope broke. Moby Dick was free and the boat stopped moving. The men sat for a minute with open mouths. Then some of them jumped into the ocean. They swam around the boat and tried to find Captain Ahab. But they couldn't see him and after some time they climbed back into the boat.

Then I heard a shout: "The ship!"

I looked around and saw the *Pequod*. There was only one sail above the water now. Queequeg was at the top of the sail and his harpoon was in his hand. He put his hand up high.

The *Pequod* went down. I saw my friend Queequeg one last time before the ship went under the water.

When a ship goes down, it takes the water with it. The water pulled the whaling boat with all the men under the water. And it pulled me nearer.

"Queequeg, am I going to meet you? Am I going to die with you?" I asked.

But then the ocean was quiet.

Suddenly something came up under me and hit me. Was it

Moby Dick again? Was it a shark? No. It was Queequeg's coffin! My dear friend helped me one last time! The coffin came to the top of the water and I climbed onto it.

♦

I stayed on Queequeg's coffin for two days and two nights. I was in the middle of the ocean with only the sky above me and water around me. My mouth was very dry and my face and arms were red from the sun. The nights were as cold as winter. Why didn't the sharks eat me? Why didn't the strong winds come and throw me into the ocean? Why didn't Moby Dick kill me?

Then I saw it—one small sail at the end of the world. It slowly came nearer and after some hours I could see the ship. The men on the ship saw me in the water and shouted at their captain. They were excited. They were happy!

When the ship came nearer, I understood. It was the *Rachel*. The men started to pull me out of the water and saw their mistake. I wasn't their captain's son. But they were very kind to me. They gave me food and water, and a bed.

♦

I often think about my time on the *Pequod*. We fought with Moby Dick, and Captain Ahab's men died. They died because one man hated a whale. At the same time the men on the *Rachel* looked for a boy. They looked for a boy because one man loved his son. And after their hard work and their hopes they found only me.

So I lived. I can tell you my story. And Moby Dick lives. He is out there now.

ACTIVITIES

Chapters 1–3

Before you read

1 Look at the Word List at the back of the book. Answer these questions with words from the Word List.

    a How big are whales?

    b What do we get from whales?

    c What do whalers use when they kill whales?

    d What other dangerous animal lives in the ocean?

2 Which word from the Word List (on the left) do you often use with a word on the right. Write one or two sentences with the two words.

    a *sail*   rich

    b *death*   ocean

    c *dream*   die

    d *star*   sleep

    e *gold*   sky

3 Read the Introduction to the book and the first five sentences from Chapter 1 and answer the questions.

    a Who or what is Moby Dick?

    b How does Captain Ahab feel about Moby Dick? Why?

    c Who is Ishmael?

    d How do you think Ishmael feels about Moby Dick? Why?

    e Do you think this story will be:

        funny? exciting? a love story? d sad?

While you read

4 What happens first? What happens next? Write the numbers 1–7.

    a Ishmael meets Starbuck.   .....

    b Starbuck and Captain Ahab fight.   .....

    c Ishmael and Queequeg get jobs on the *Pequod*. .....

    d The whalers meet Captain Ahab.   .....

    e Ishmael goes to Nantucket.   .....

    f Ishmael finds a whaling ship.   .....

    g Ishmael meets Queequeg.   .....

After you read

5 Who are these people? What do you know about them?

    a Queequeg   **e** Bildad, Tashtego, Daggoo, Flask,

    b Elijah   and Manxman

    c Starbuck   **f** Pip

    d Stubb

6 Why:

    a does Ishmael go to the *Pequod* and not to another ship?

    b doesn't Captain Ahab come up and meet the sailors?

    c is whaling a hard life?

    d does Ishmael want to go whaling?

    e does Starbuck say, "Please Captain. Stop."

    f do Starbuck and Captain Ahab fight?

    g does Pip get angry with Ishmael?

Chapters 4–6

Before you read

7 Discuss these questions. What do you think?

    a Pip is right. There are men below. Who are these men?

    b What happens when a whaling ship finds a whale?

While you read

8 Are these sentences right (R) or wrong (W)?

    a A whale hits one of the *Pequod's* whaling boats.   .....

    b Some whalers have a bad night on the ocean.   .....

    c We learn about Starbuck's family.   .....

    d The captain of another ship helps Captain Ahab

       look for Moby Dick.   .....

    e The *Pequod* catches Moby Dick.   .....

    f Moby Dick kills a man.   .....

After you read

9 Who says these things? Who or what are they talking about?

    a "These were Ahab's devils!"

    b "Is he forgetting his wife and child?"

    c "Nobody's waiting for me."

d "*Leave* him!"

e "Does he have the eyes of a cat?"

f "Crazy old man."

10 Finish these sentences.

    a The whalers have to cut the fat off the whales quickly because …

    b Money isn't important to Captain Ahab because …

    c Fedallah watches for Moby Dick at night because …

    d Some whalers think Captain Ahab listens to Fedallah because …

    e Ishmael is afraid of Captain Ahab because …

11 Work with another student. Have one of these conversations.

    a *Student A*: You are Ishmael and you are afraid. Why are you afraid? What do you think will happen? Tell Starbuck.

    Student B: You are Starbuck. Listen to Ishmael and ask questions. Don't tell him that you are afraid too.

    b *Student A*: You are Captain Boomer. You are on the *Samuel Enderby* after your visit to the *Pequod*. Tell another man on your ship about your visit.

    Student B: You work on the *Samuel Enderby*. Ask Captain Boomer questions about the *Pequod* and Captain Ahab.

Chapters 7–8

Before you read

12 Look at the names of Chapters 7 and 8 on the Contents page at the front of the book. Discuss these questions.

    a What is going to happen to Pip?

    b Why do you think Queequeq has a coffin?

While you read

13 Write a word in each sentence.

    a Pip has to go on his first whaling trip because another man …………… his arm.

    b On the second trip Pip …………… out of the boat.

    c On the third trip Stubb …………… Pip in the ocean.

d After that, Pip . . . . that Captain Ahab is God.

e Captain Ahab doesn't want to . . . . the ship and change the barrels.

f Queequeg is strong, so he . . . . a lot of the hard work.

g Queequeg asks for a coffin because he is going to . . . .

h After some days Queequeg . . . . better and goes to work again.

After you read

14 Discuss these questions. Why:

    a does Stubb leave Pip in the ocean? Do you think he is right?

    b does Pip go crazy? Can you understand this?

    c is Captain Ahab kind to Pip?

    d does Captain Ahab stop the ship for Starbuck?

    e does Queequeg think he is going to die?

Chapters 9–10

Before you read

15 In Chapter 9 Captain Ahab dreams about his future. What do you think he dreams? Why does he tell Fedallah about the dream?

16 Read the first six sentences of Chapter 10. What do you think is going to happen next?

While you read

17 Why do these things happen? Write one of these words next to each sentence.

wind   boy   time   dream   sharks   future

    a The whalers watch the four whales.   . . . . .

    b Captain Ahab is afraid.   . . . . .

    c Captain Ahab asks Fedallah about his dream.   . . . . .

    d Starbuck wants Captain Ahab to turn back.   . . . . .

    e Captain Gardiner wants to find his boat.   . . . . .

    f Captain Ahab doesn't help Captain Gardiner.   . . . . .

Now write full sentences with the same words.

    a The whalers watch the four whales because . . .

18 Why are these things important to the story?
- **a** a rope
- **d** Ahab's room
- **b** maps
- **e** a bird
- **c** a gun

19 Discuss these questions.
- **a** "Now I understood!" Who thinks this? Why? Do you think some people can see the future?
- **b** Why does Starbuck want to kill Captain Ahab? Why doesn't he kill him? Do you think he is right?

Chapters 11–13

Before you read

20 You are going to read about the big fight with Moby Dick. What do you think happens in the fight to:

Captain Ahab?   Fedallah?   Ishmael?   Moby Dick?

While you read

21 Do these things happen on the 1st, 2nd or 3rd day of the fight?
- **a** Captain Ahab uses a harpoon for a leg.   .....
- **b** Three of the boats break.   .....
- **c** Captain Ahab sees Moby Dick first.   .....
- **d** Moby Dick hits the *Pequod*.   .....
- **e** Fedallah dies.   .....
- **f** Moby Dick breaks Captain Ahab's boat.   .....
- **g** The men see Fedallah's body.   .....
- **h** Some of the men's harpoons hit Moby Dick.   .....
- **i** Ishmael finds Queequeg's coffin.   .....

After you read

22 Have a conversation between Ishmael and a friend after the end of the story.

Student A: You are the friend. Ask Ishmael questions. What happened on the ocean? How does Ishmael feel now? What is he going to do in the future?

Student B: You are Ishmael. Answer your friend's questions.

Writing

23 You are Ishmael. Write a story for a magazine about your time on the *Pequod* and the famous white whale, Moby Dick.

24 Do you feel sorry for Captain Ahab, or angry with him? Why? What kind of man was he before he met Moby Dick? Write about him.

25 What do you think happens to Ishmael after his time on the *Pequod*? Does he find a wife? Where does he live? Does he work on a whaling ship again? Why (not)? Write about his life.

26 You are Ishmael. Write a letter to Queequeg's father in Kokovoko and tell him about your time on the *Pequod*. Tell him about his son's death. Tell him that Queequeg was a good friend.

27 Fedallah and Queequeg could see the future. Would you like to see the future? Do you think this is a good thing or a bad thing?

28 What did you learn about a whaler's life when you read *Moby Dick*? Why did men want to be whalers? Why was it a dangerous job?

29 Write a conversation between two of the *Pequod*'s whalers before they die. How do they feel about their life on the ship? How do they feel about Captain Ahab, Starbuck, and Fedallah and his men?

30 Tell another famous story about life on the ocean.